Catherine
Bagnall &
L. Jane Sayle

on we go

MASSEY UNIVERSITY PRESS

To Julian Bishop,
who made all the difference.

Contents

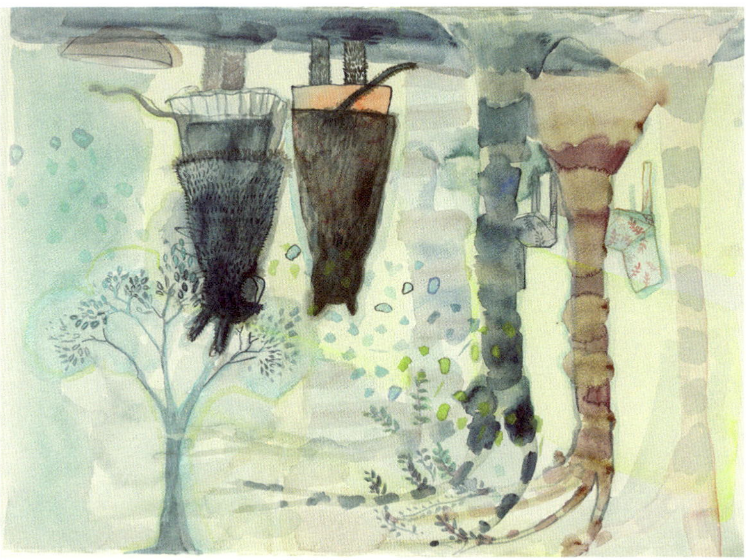

The time of the now

How to hear the rumble and echo
of the world
and refuse to understand it
it's not what you think
the right now
dwelling in the way of it

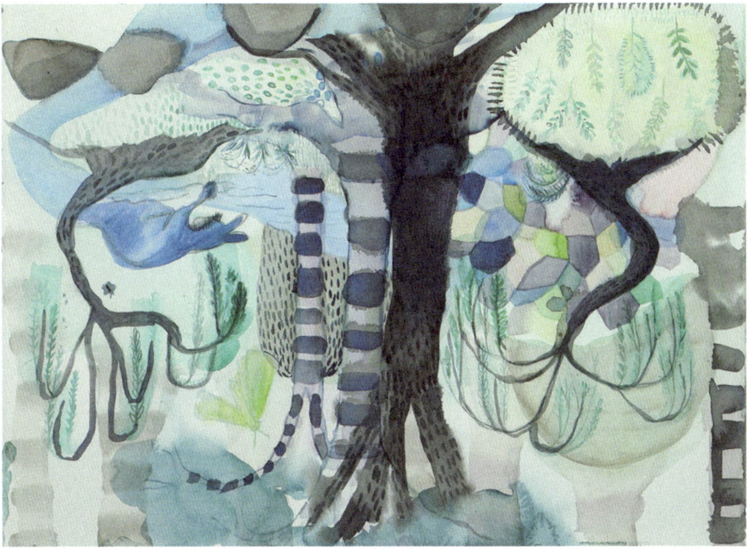

Overwhelmed by something
and happy to be
because of the mystery
and the plenitude

Deep tunnels in white cliffs
craquelure on the black square
who knows what they may mean?
I just love the big feeling

It's springtime for the lone sentry
on guard at his outpost and musing
on happiness
a primary school word
that doesn't begin to explain
the charms of living he thought

The first day

The invisible birds call their sudden joy
across the peaked façades of silhouette buildings
whose windows bulge with a molten yellow light
that yearns for the poised evening air
more than yesterday

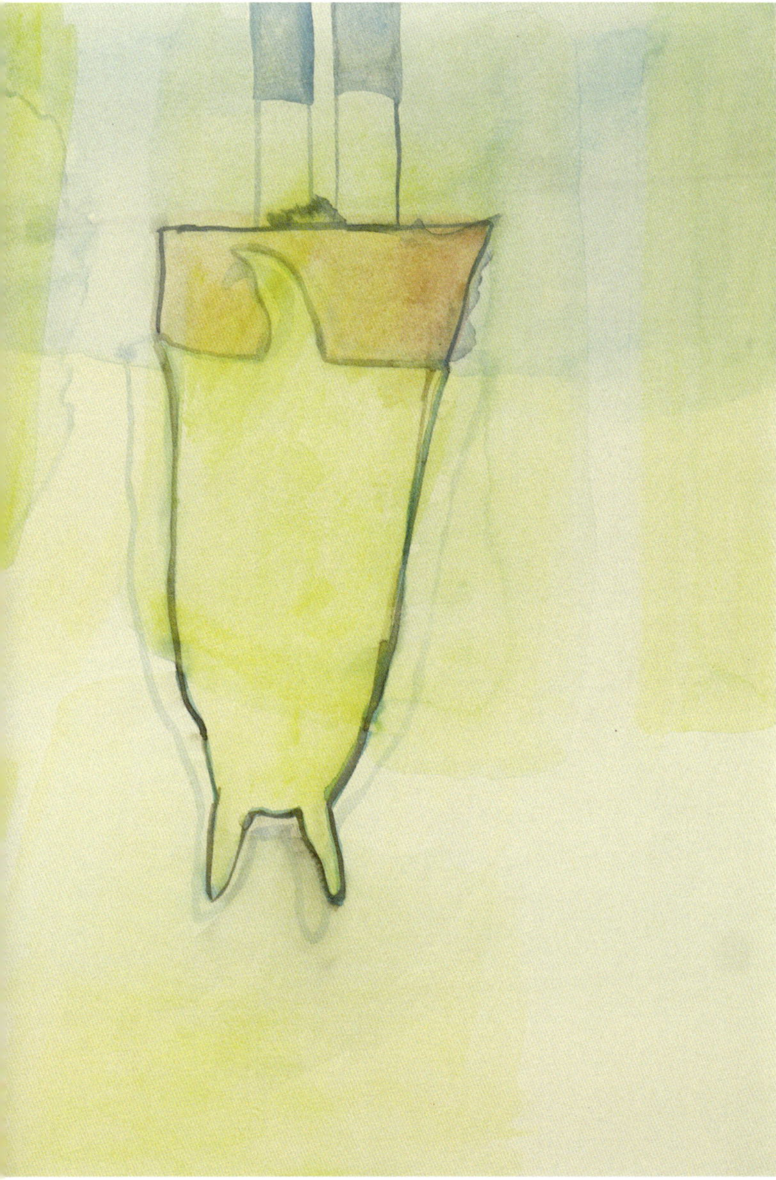

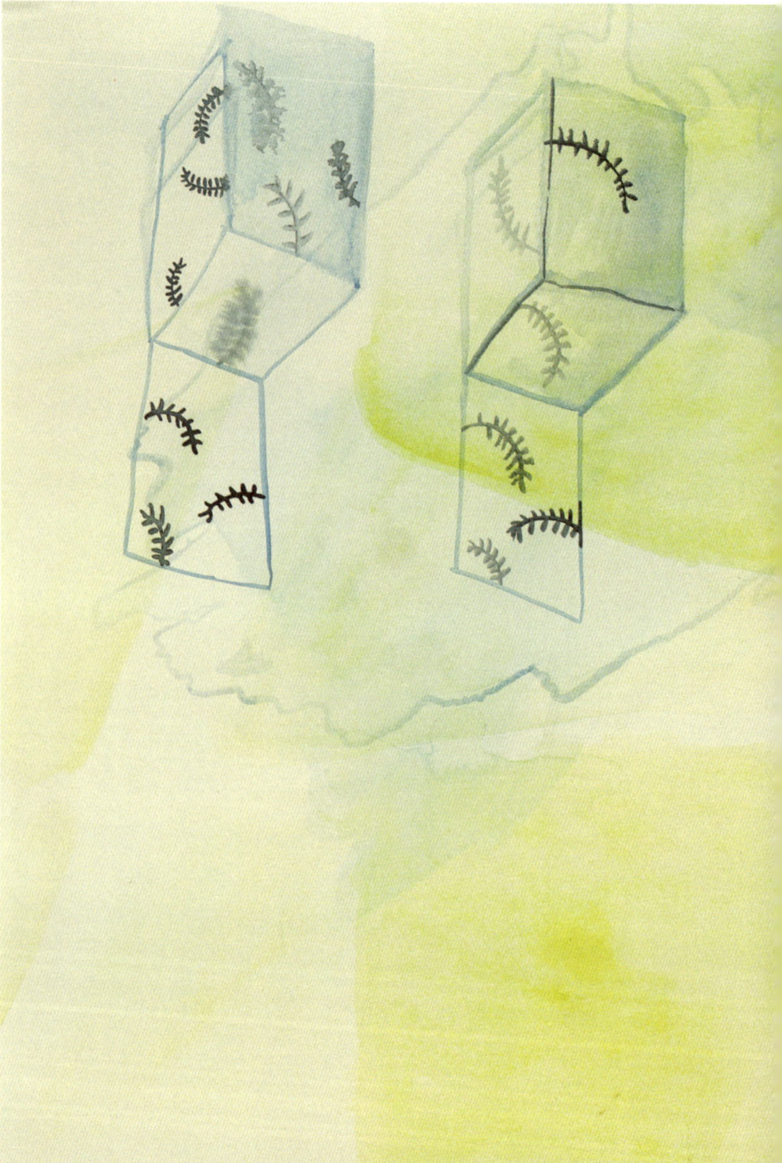

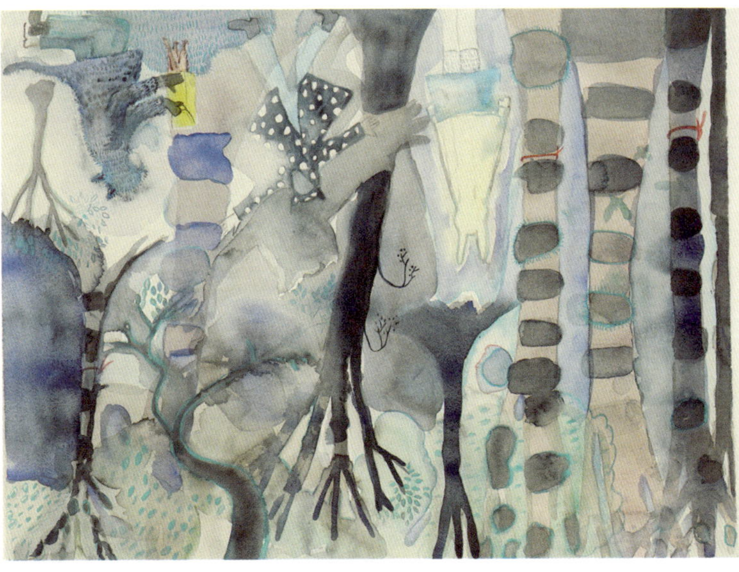

At last

If you stand outside
and stretch out your arms
the falling snow
will beautify you

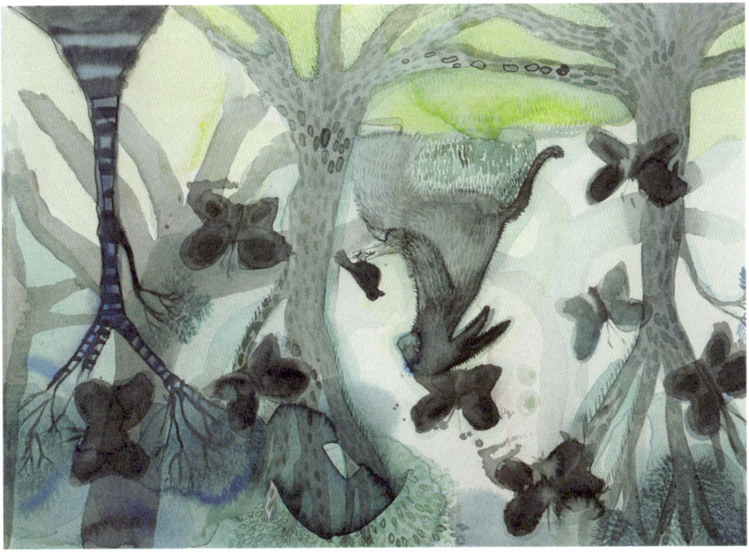

What bird is that?

Between winds
soft sunshine
strands of lemon lichen
across a satin-grey rock bank
and the smell of blackberry
living for the moment
inside the quiet air
on the nameless day

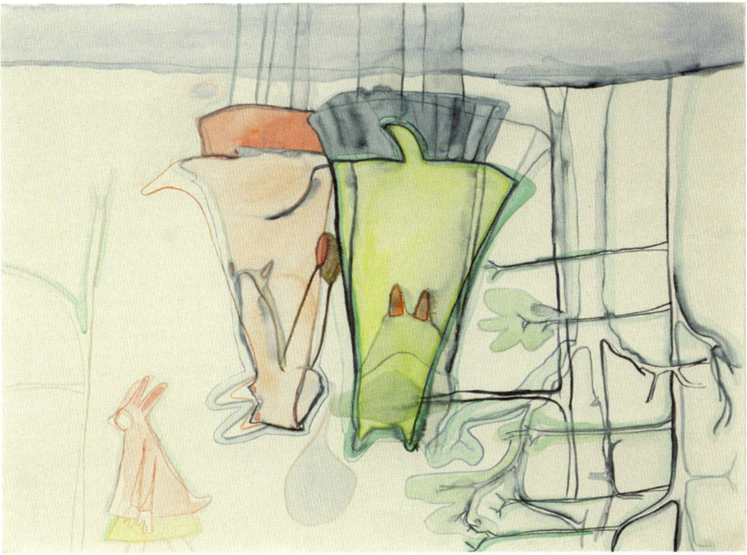

On we go

Empty suitcase made of leaves
and a stomach light as air
just to walk up in the sky
talking with you

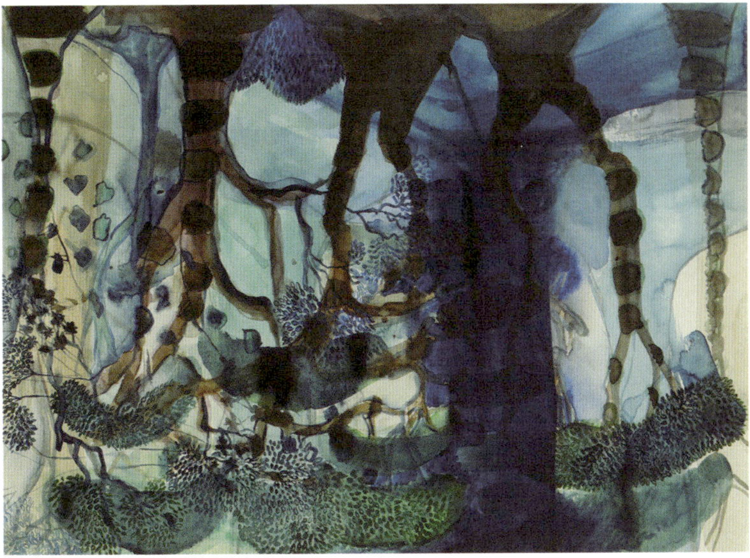

Companions

We were out of business
and approximate
as the city calmly froze

That night
by the side of a deserted road
glistening black wolves
slipped in the shadows
and quietly
the tall trees in the dark forest beyond

Going back

Though we were long gone
all our coats were hanging
on hooks in the hall

How things wait
for us to come back
how they mutely love us
as they fade

It's only easy to let go
because you've known
the ancient loving warmth
of a small chapel
hewn into living rock
and lit with a hundred candles

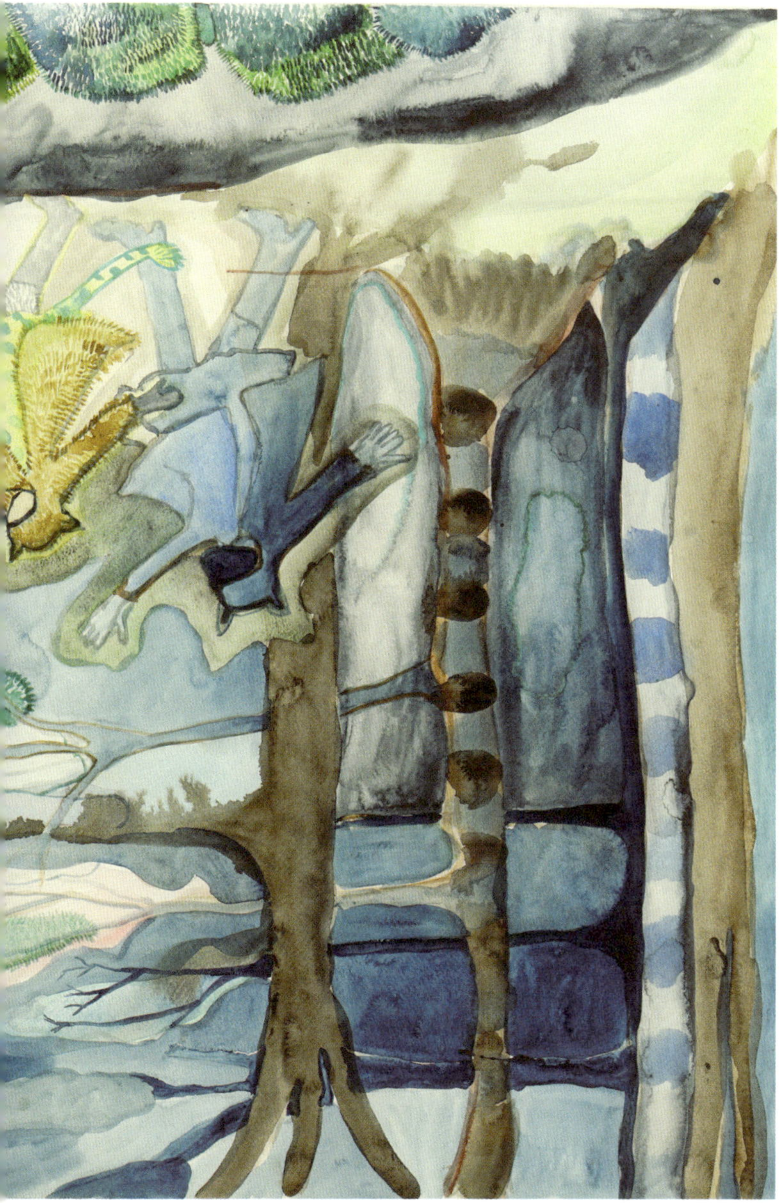

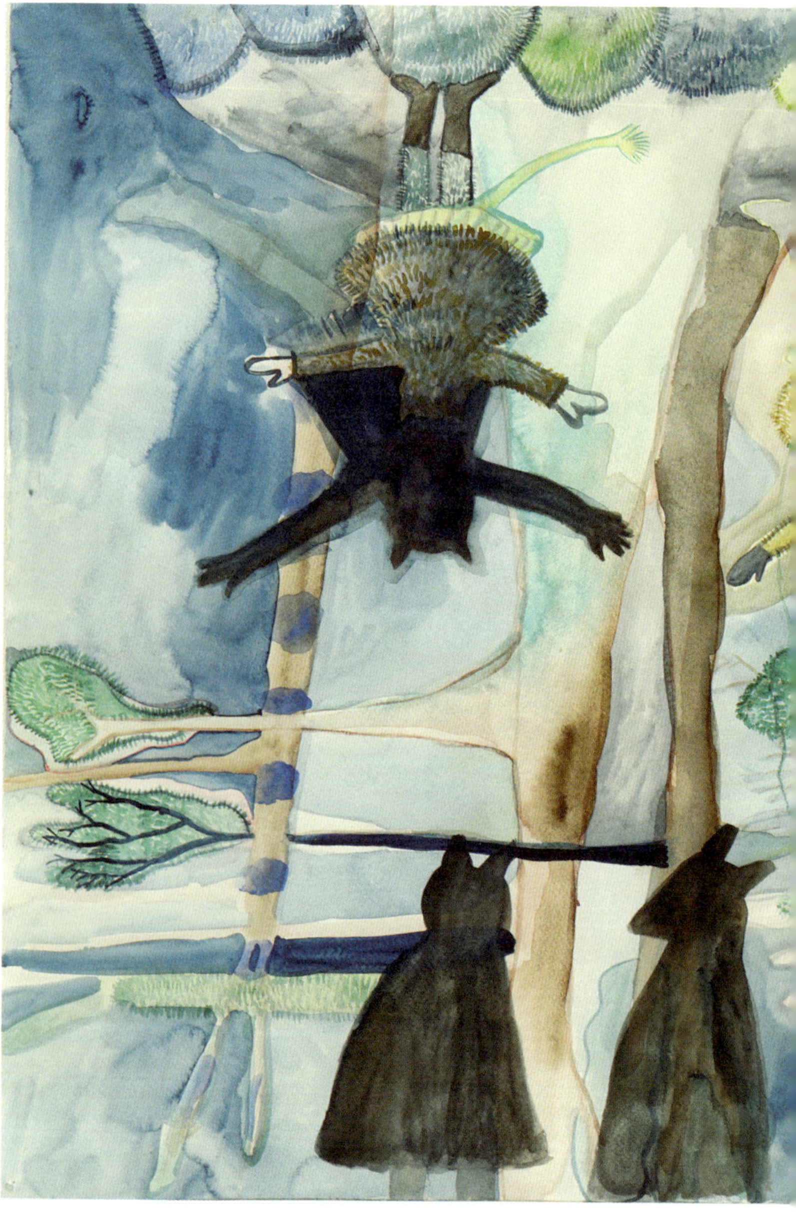

Lovey

Among the leaves
a blackbird
frisks itself clean
in the steady rain

We could have sat quietly
without effort or heart shape
and watched together
if you were still here

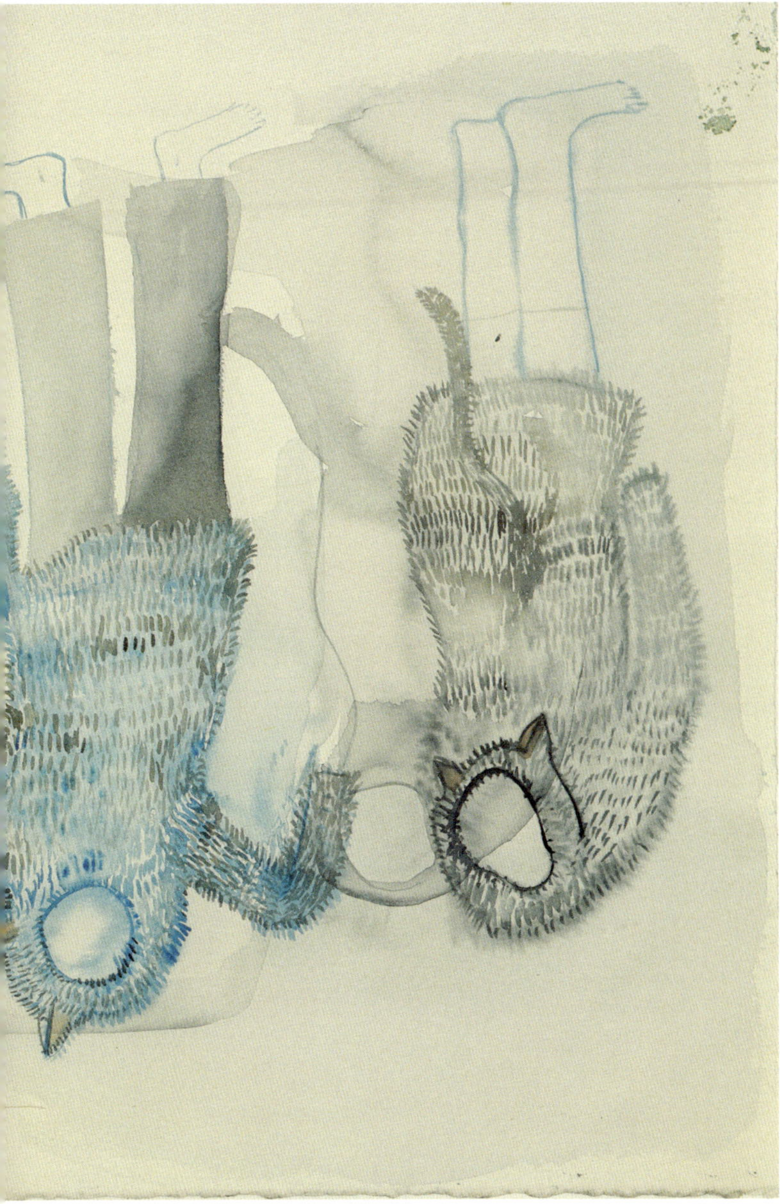

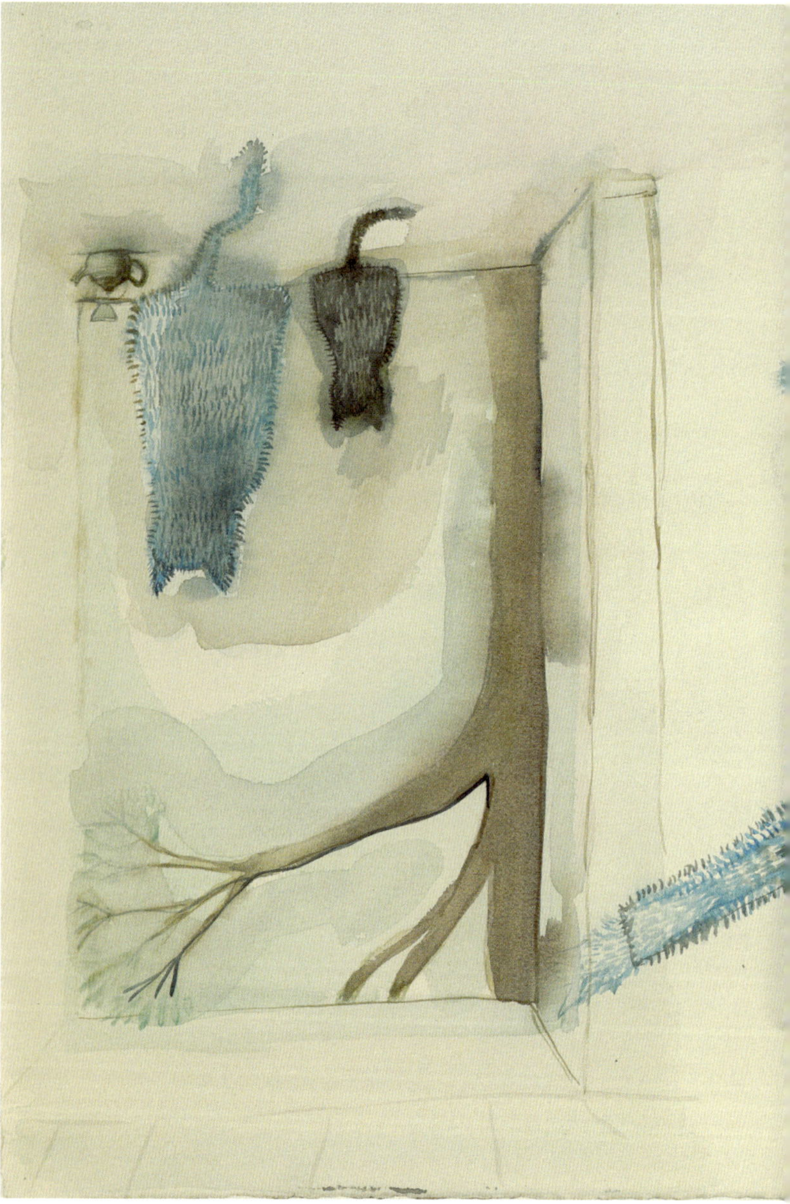

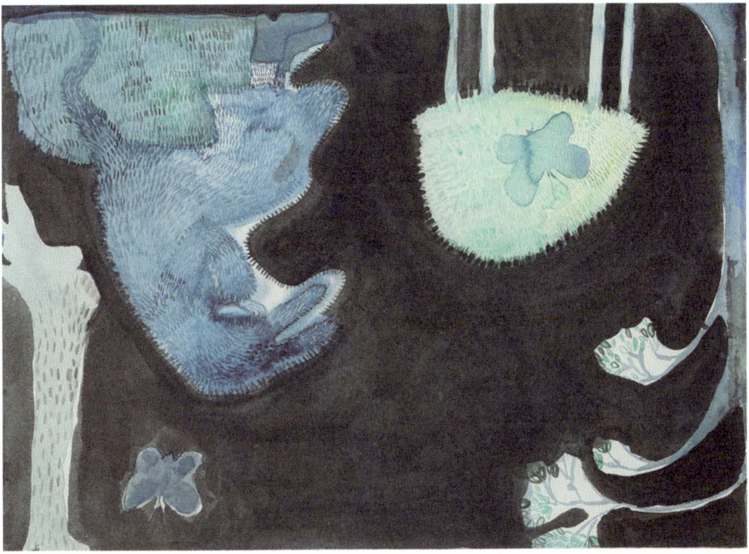

In my stomach a winter garden at night
through infinities of dark space
constellations glitter and whirl in my head
as wrong worlds of dream
unfurl into waking hours
and gleam
and stay as close

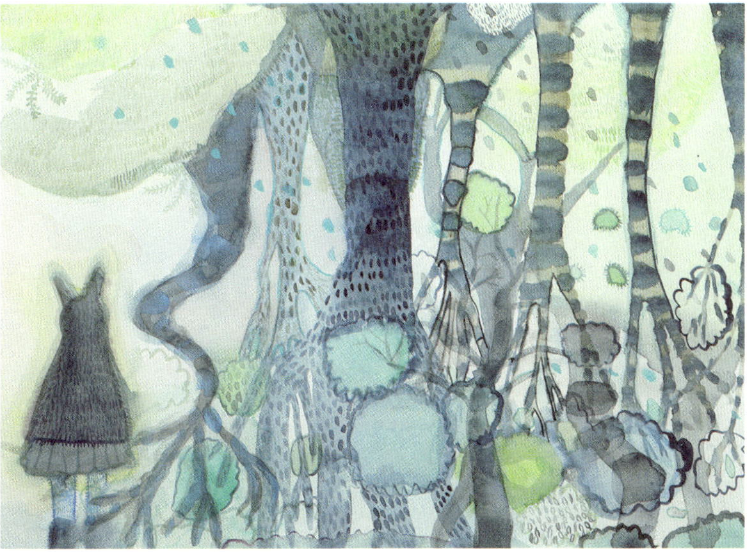

Botanical

In the early morning greying
of the moonless night
eyes open green
and I know where it is
the secret bamboo grove

Better than houses
the old *Tilia*
a dome world of bright leaves

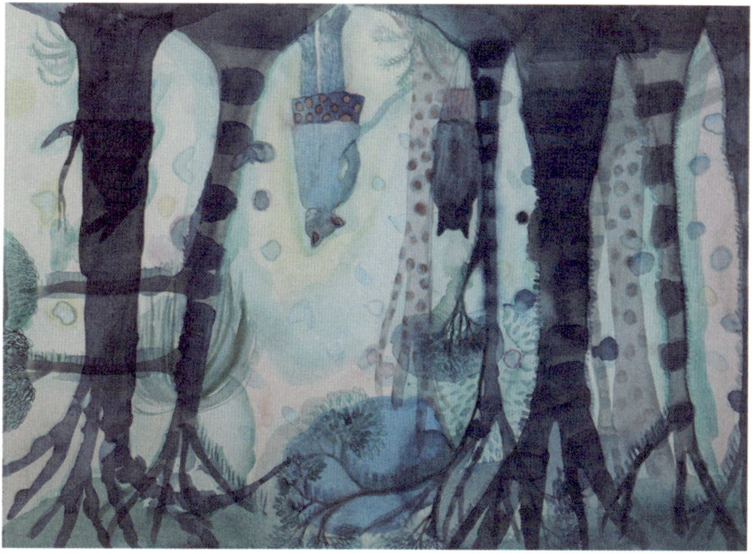

As you were

You seem to do a better job
of living inside me
than out in the world
at large as you were

You came by near dawn
a small glowing figure
wandering through deep black space
as if through a garden

how did all this light find its way into you
and don't you mind the endless night?

Bedtime

We sleep well here
in Cloudy land
two narrow duvets
and eighty white centimetres
of cloud
in each pillowcase

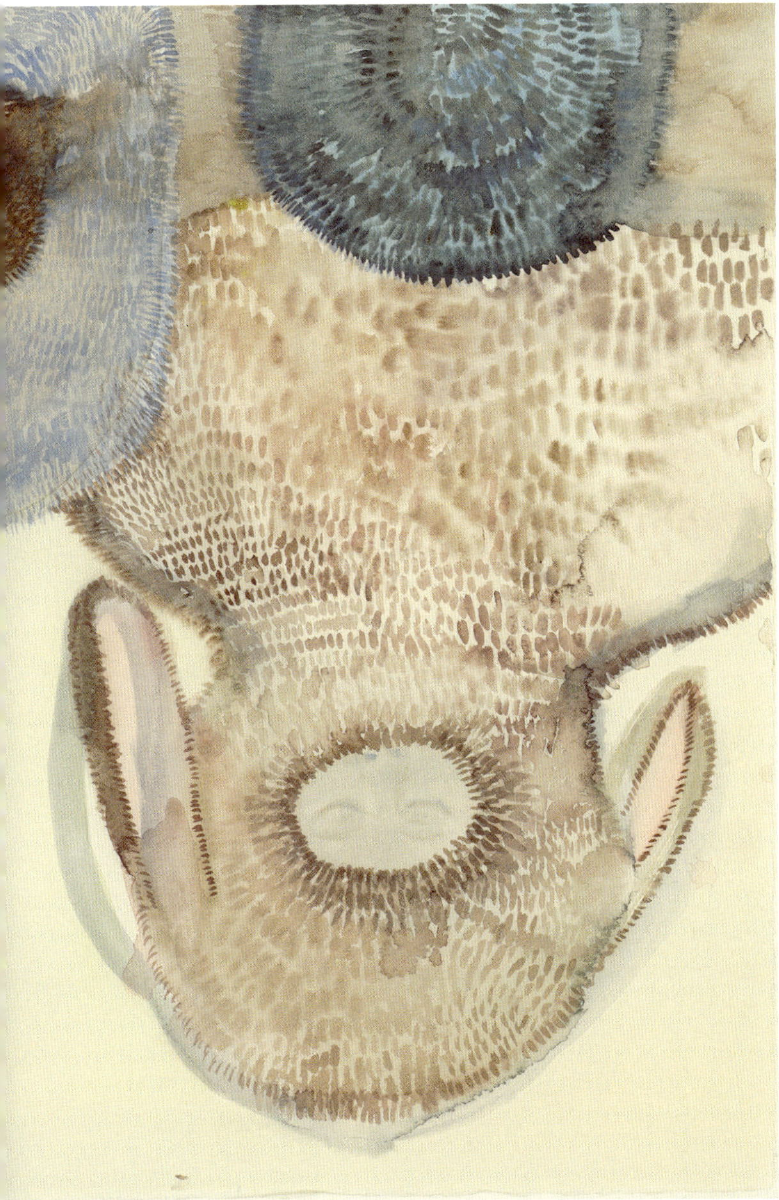

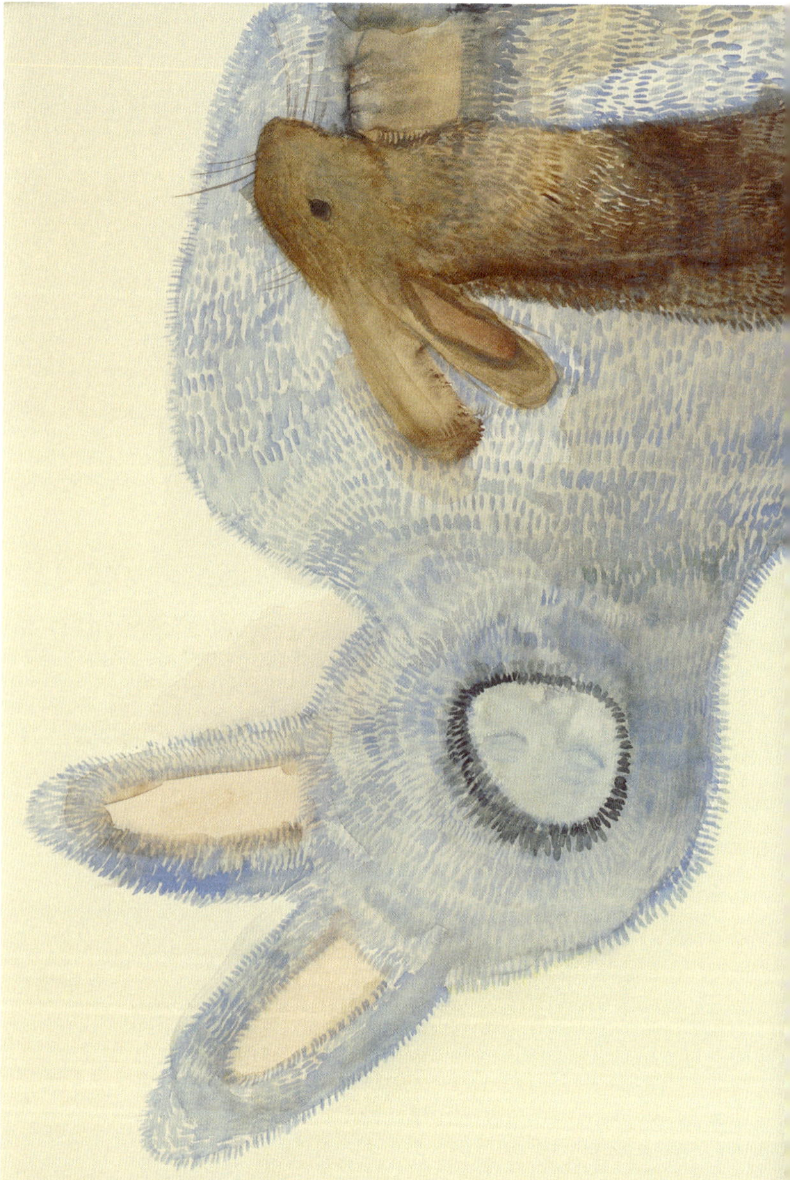

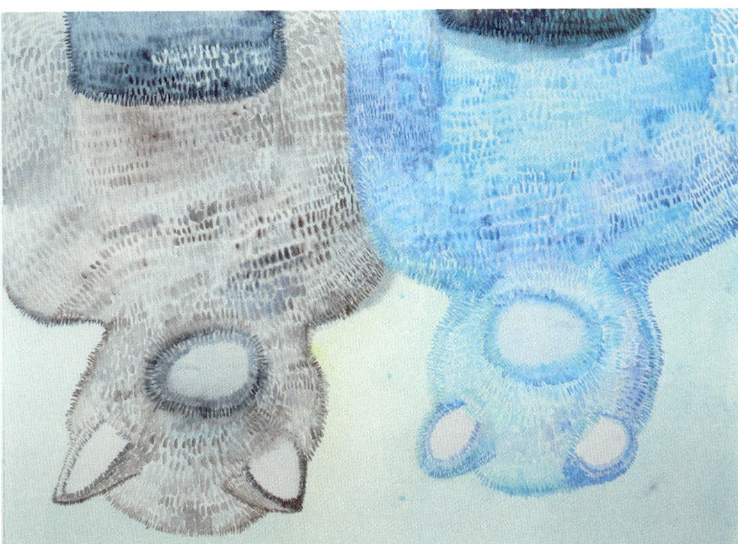

The company

A rabbit under the pillow
birds in the bed

But I'm still in my winter
me and my snowman friends!

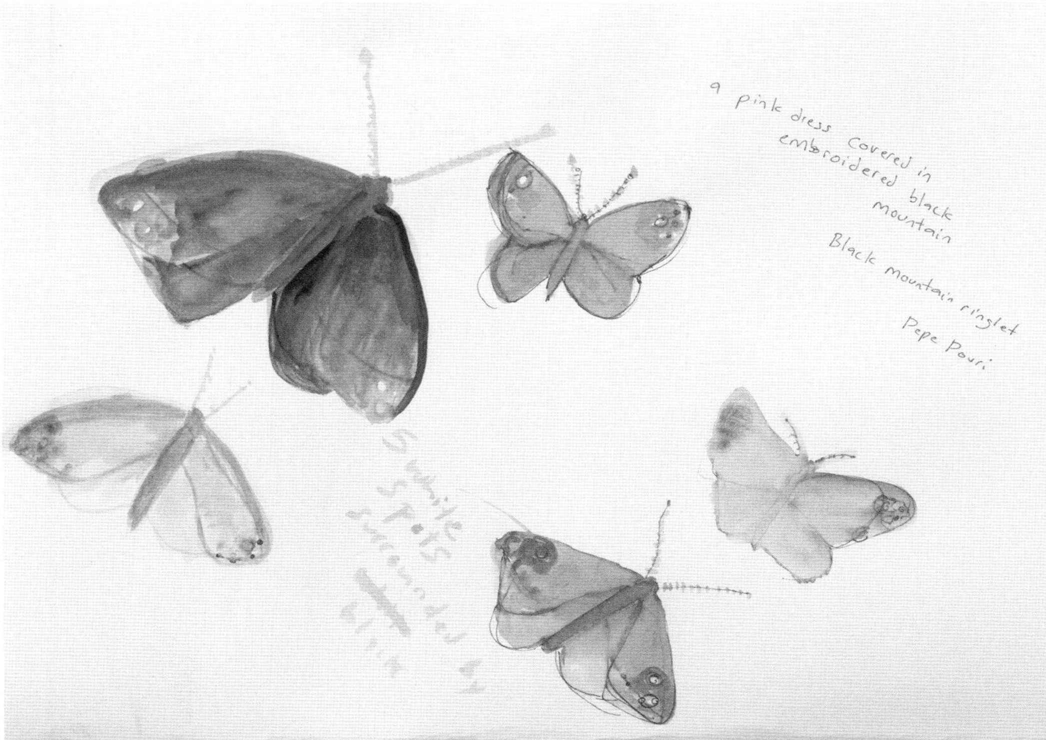
9 pink dress covered in
embroidered black
mountain
Black mountain ringlet
Pepe Pouri
5 white
spots
surrounded by
pink

An ember-winged monarch
breathes in and out
the shadow of daylight

Between the swirling night
and the dark hills and creeks
of the inchoate past
permanent private energy

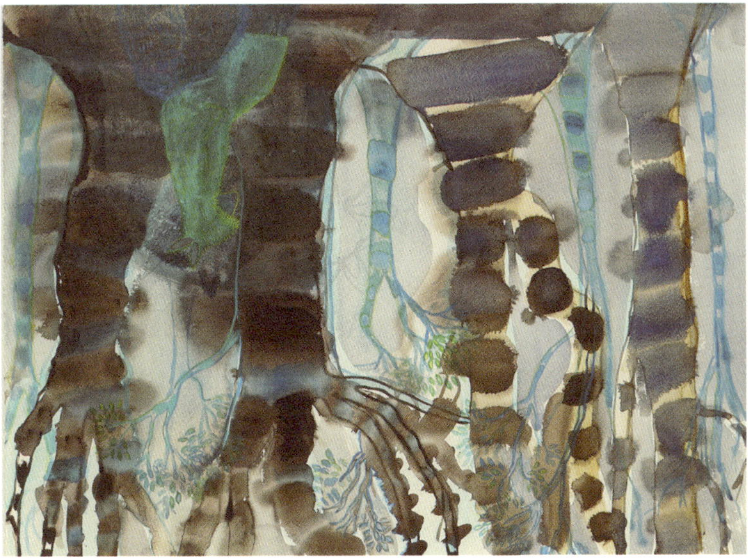

Souvenir

Places of permanent shadow
live here
and hand-sized pieces of fear
mottle daytime things

At night
along winding empty streets
black mirror windows
face shadow pavements
and from depthless gardens
the wind roaring inside your head

360 degrees

Now boys, listen
the plan is diaphanous
and crunchy
like clear cellophane
crumpling
buoyant
catching jagged sunlight
and the sound
the sound of it!

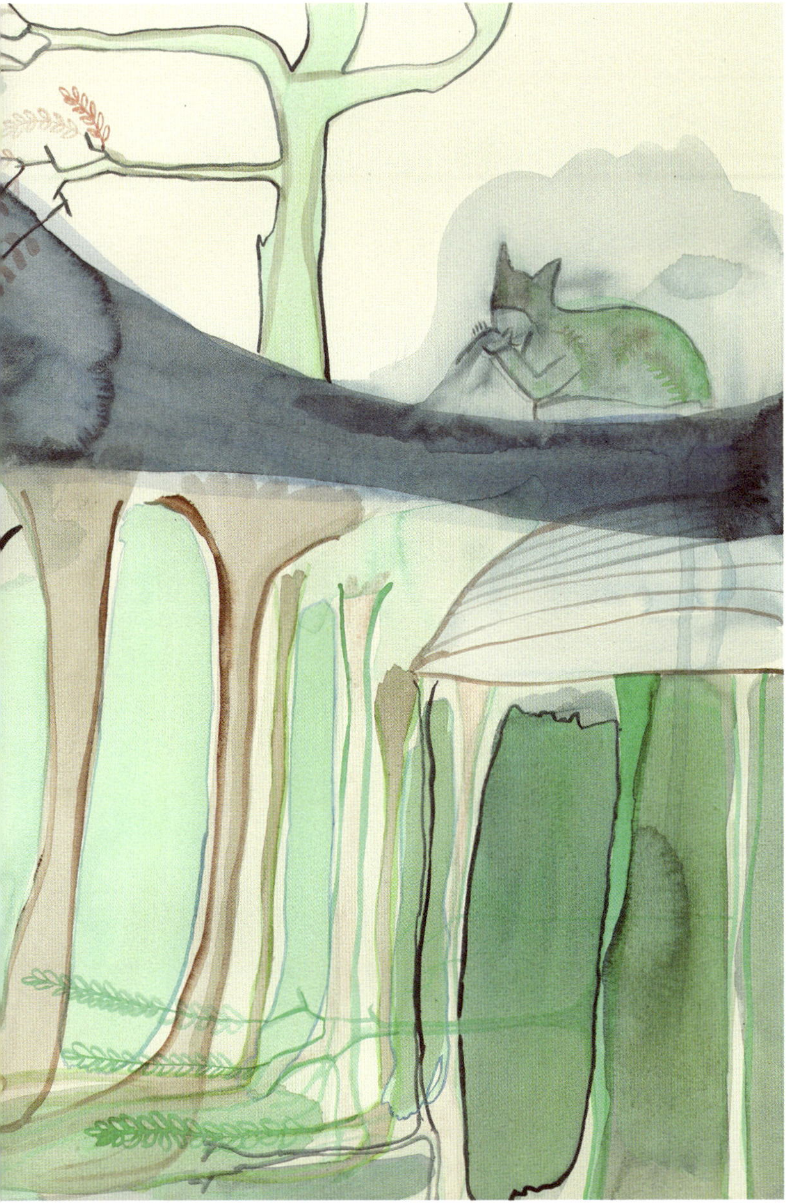

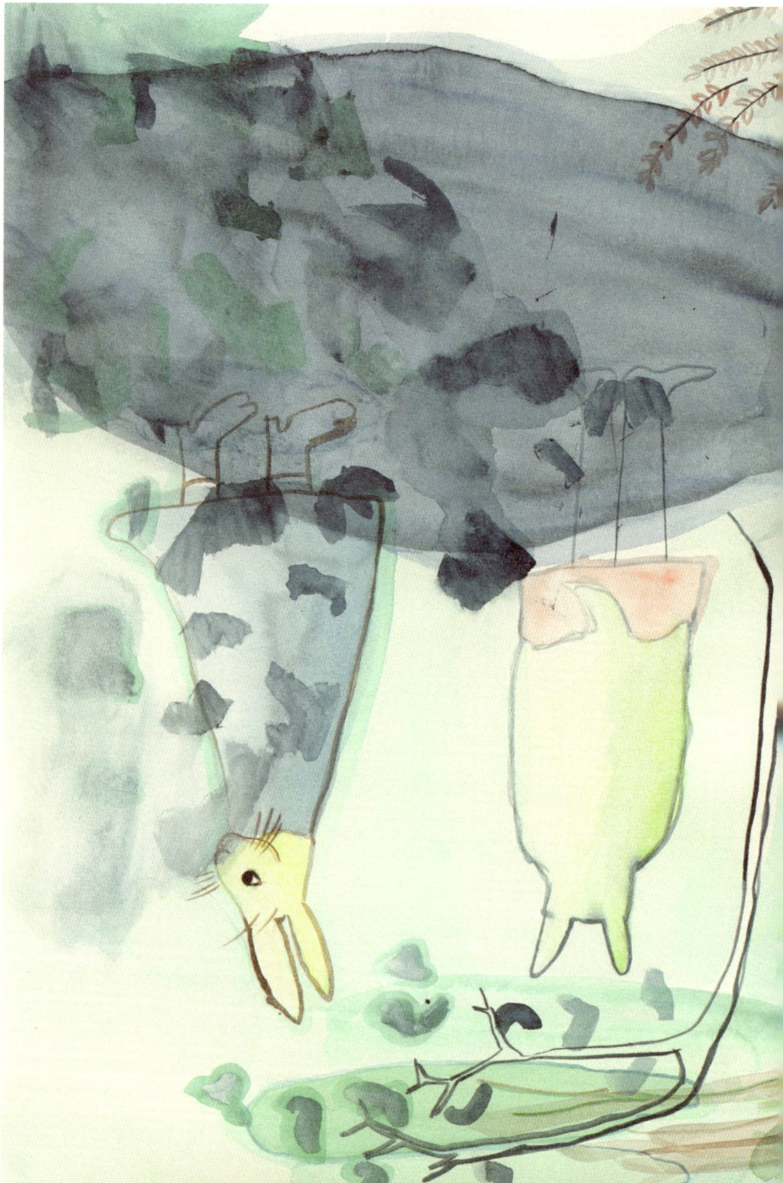

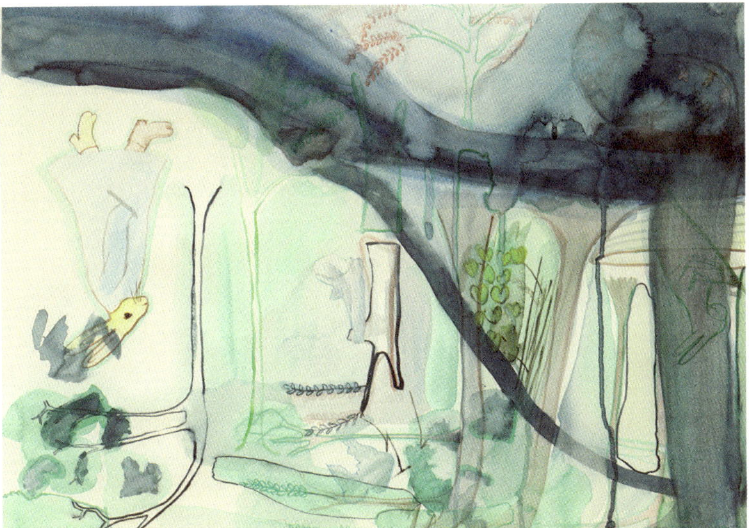

Superstructure

Spring green comes
to smother the hard lines
of this graceless town
so convincingly
I can no longer
find my way around

And it seems to me
I'm in a better world

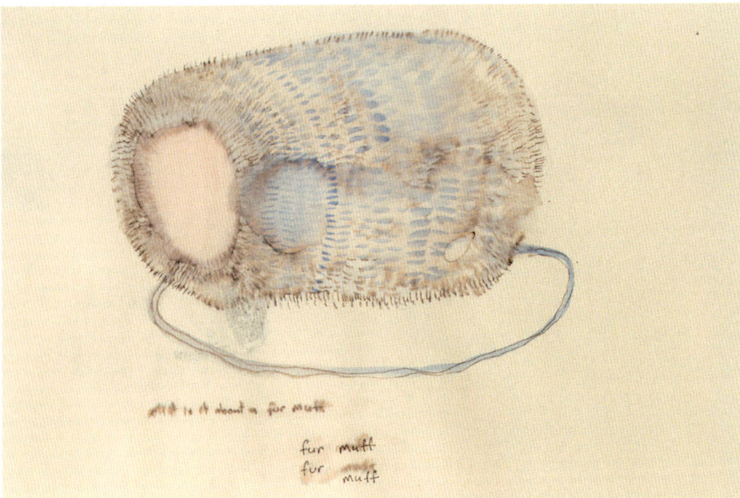
fur muff
fur muff

As to my infinite
private future
make the coffin smaller
put it on the kitchen table
and lay your loving arms over it

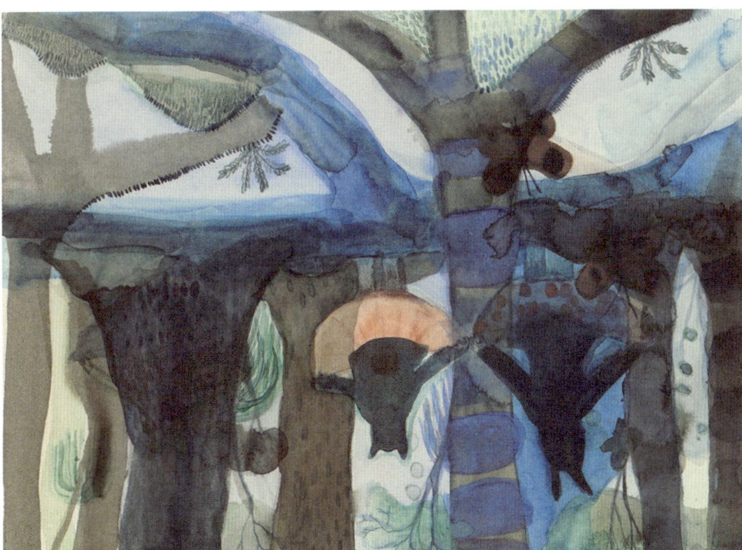

Quartz Hill

Lights out and
the small window sky
is a darkening hinterland
of smooth flinty
extraterrestrial
indiquoise

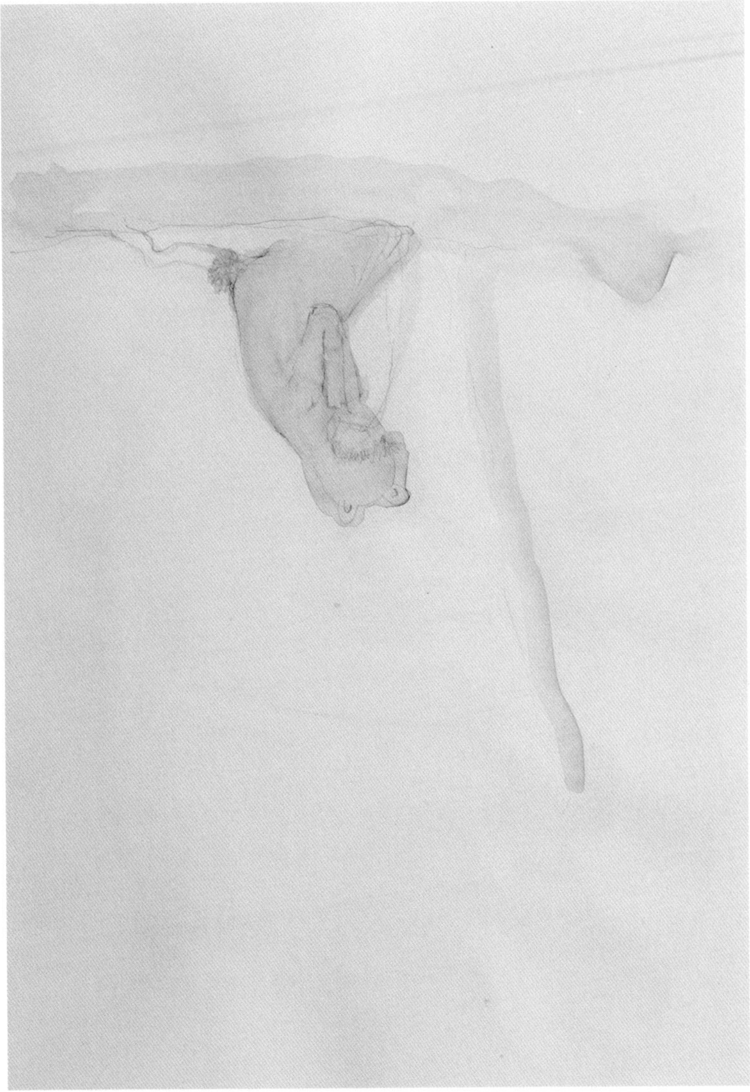

The flowers of St Francis

Prostrate and alone
in a high summer meadow
sobbing your tender heart out
but don't despair
the host of lovers to come
are waiting in the black and whiteness
behind your closed wet eyes
cry harder longer
cry more
and we will love you for it

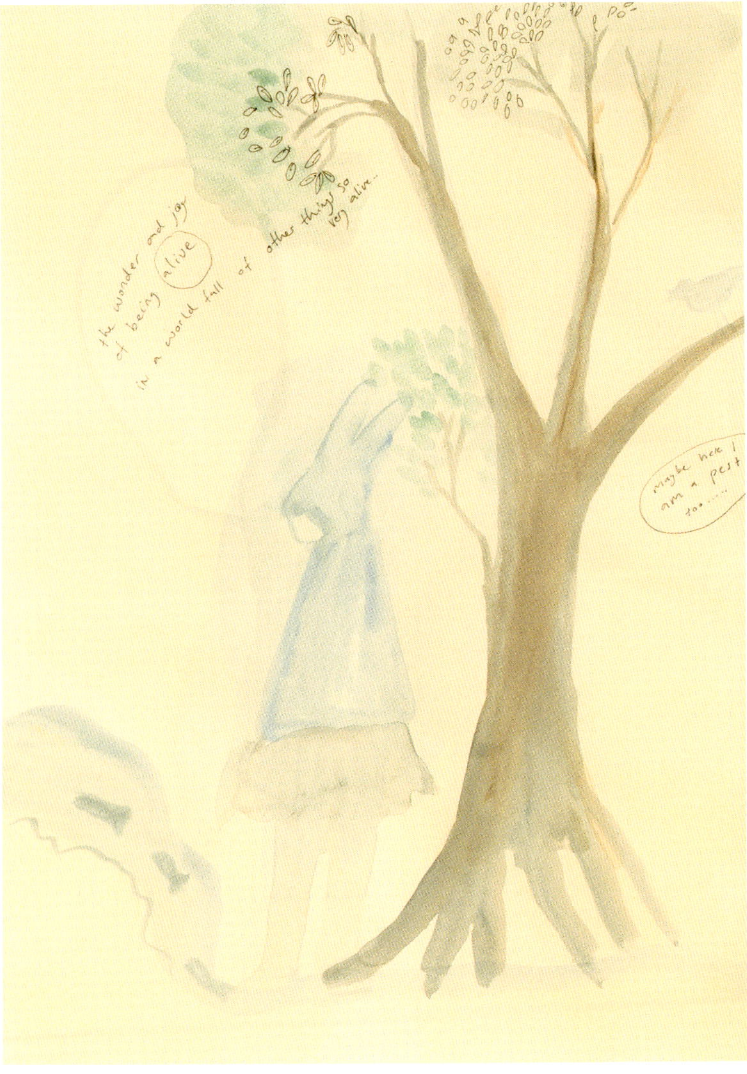
the wonder and joy
of being alive
in a world full of other things so
very alive...
maybe here I
am a pest
too......

Two heroes

Its parents knew nothing
but the baby was wise
remember the time long ago
when he said
you be brave
and I'll be free

Even with sunlight
through their leaves
the dark trees
around the old school
make it permanently mysterious

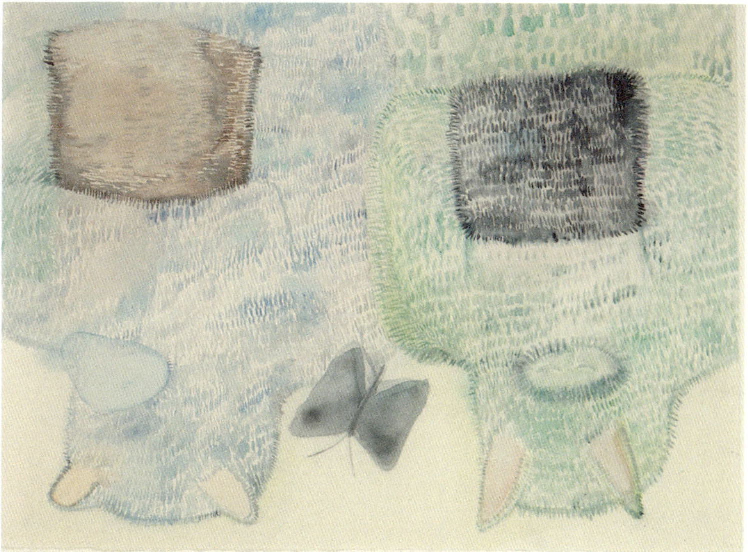

Wildflowers

Day by day
waking up
with heart beating so fast

Is it you?

List of works

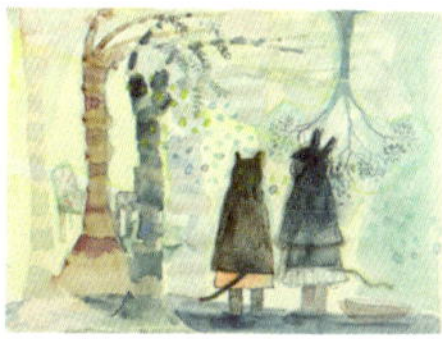

Lightness, 2013
watercolour on paper
170 x 570 mm

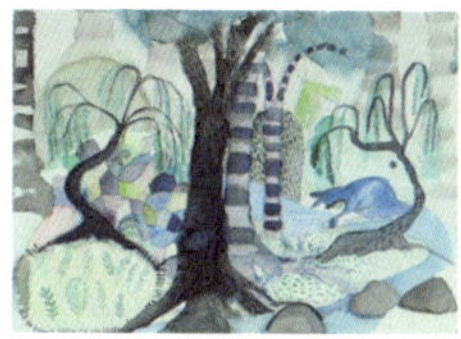

Puri puri moth, 2019
watercolour on paper
170 x 570 mm

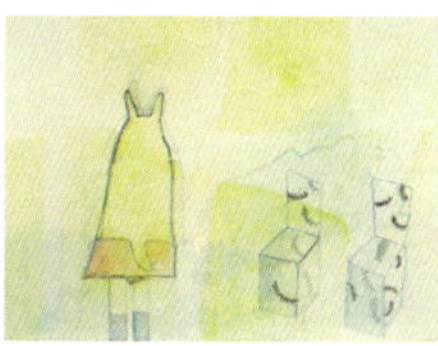

Sunlight, 2013
watercolour on paper
170 x 570 mm

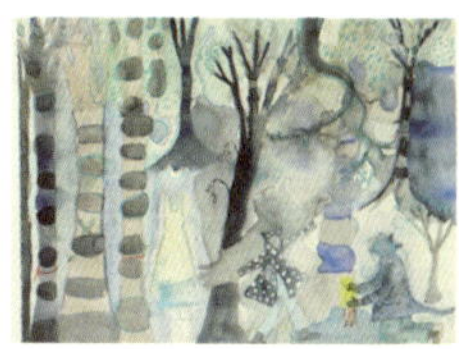

Trap-line in Gollans Valley
2016, watercolour on
paper, 170 x 570 mm

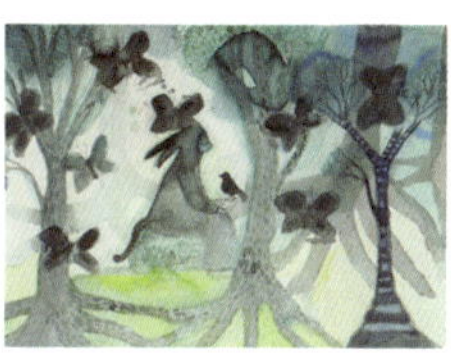

Dusk, 2018
watercolour on paper
170 x 570 mm

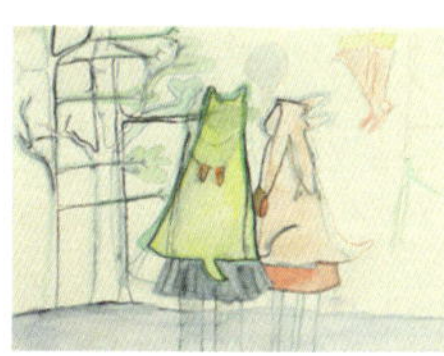

Listening with my satin ears
2013, watercolour on
paper, 170 x 570 mm

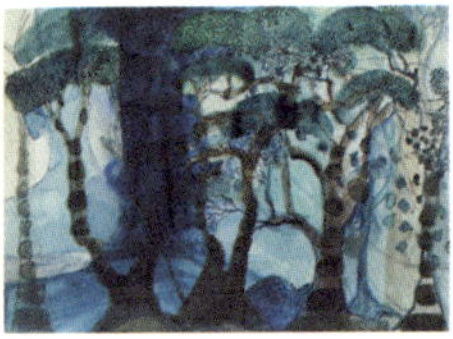

Waiting, 2018
watercolour on paper
170 x 570 mm

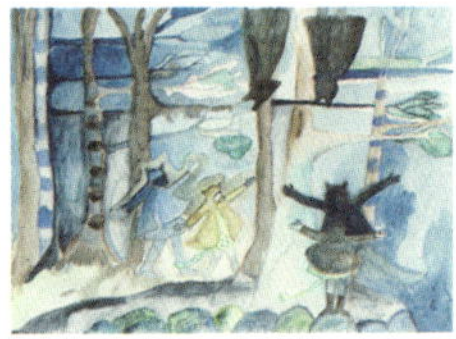

Shadows, 2018
watercolour on paper
170 x 570 mm

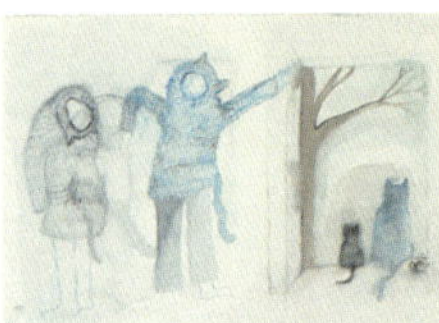

Sitting with Teddy, 2017
watercolour on paper
170 x 570 mm

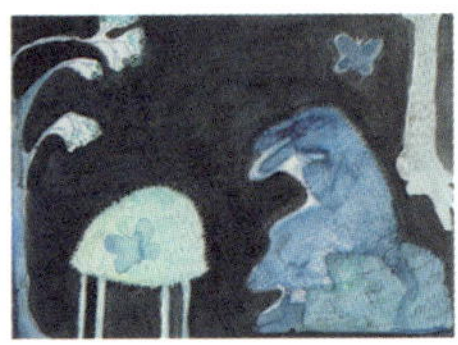

Night moth, 2017
watercolour on paper
170 x 570 mm

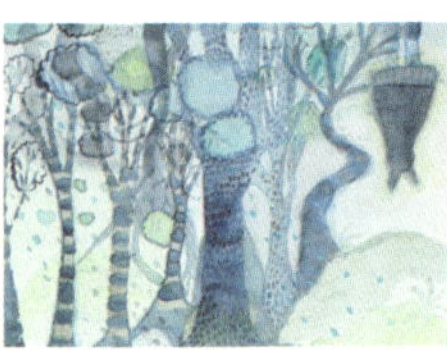

Green and stillness, 2018
watercolour on paper
170 x 570 mm

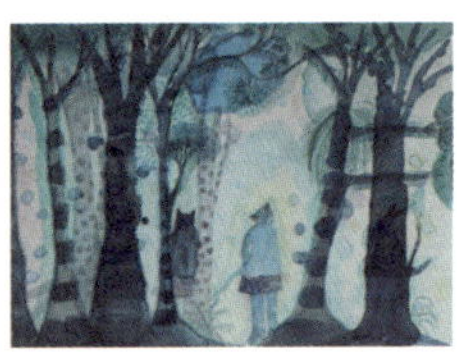

Green girl stands under the tawa trees, 2018
watercolour on paper
170 x 570 mm

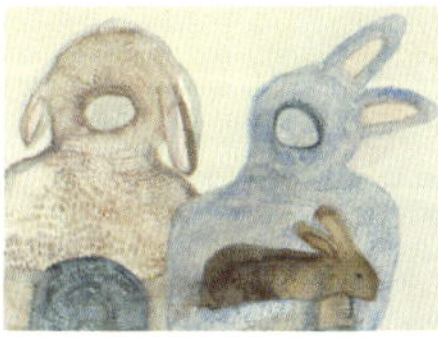

Furry things, 2020
watercolour on paper
170 x 570 mm

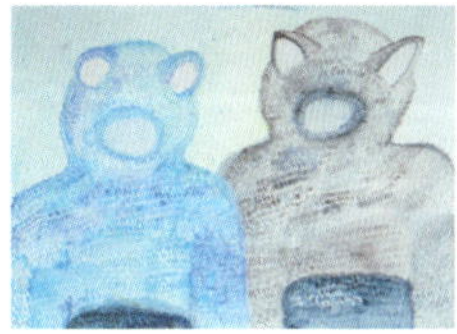

Small things, 2018
watercolour on paper
170 x 570 mm

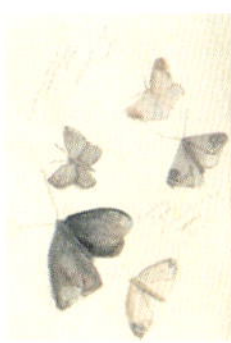

Pepi pouri, 2020
watercolour on paper
notebook page

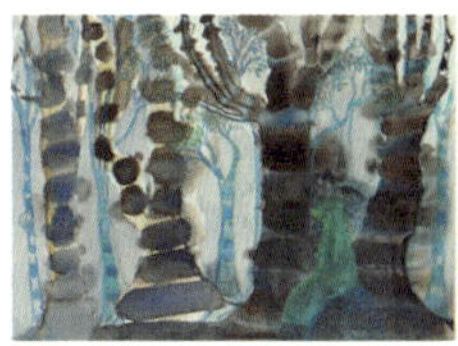

The moss girl waits, 2020
watercolour on paper
170 x 570 mm

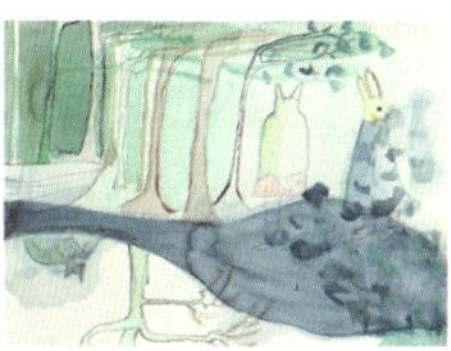

Bunny face 1, 2015
watercolour on paper
170 x 570 mm

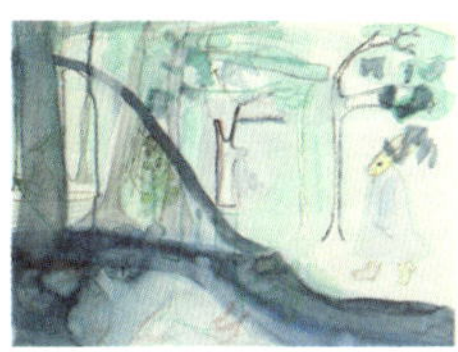

Bunny face 2, 2015
watercolour on paper
170 x 570 mm

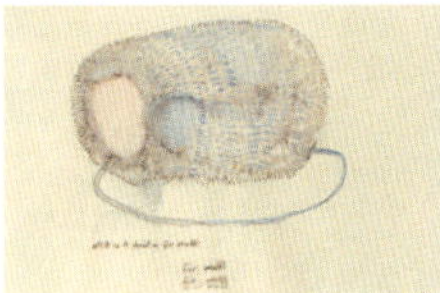

Fur muff, 2020
watercolour on paper
notebook page

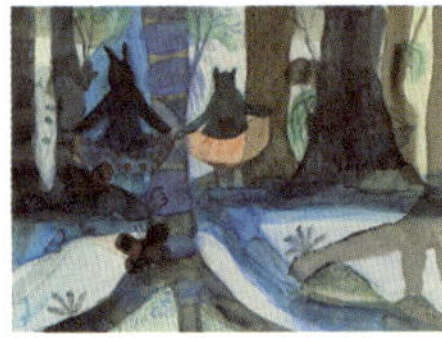

Night watching, 2020
watercolour on paper
170 x 570 mm

Weeping, 2020
watercolour on paper
notebook page

The wonder of it all, 2020
watercolour on paper
notebook page

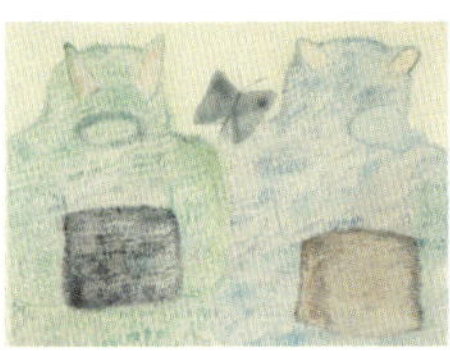

Warm days, 2017
watercolour on paper
170 x 570 mm

About the artist and the poet

CATHERINE BAGNALL grew up between the bush and the eastern shore of the Wellington harbour in New Zealand. She is an internationally recognised artist who teaches at the College of Creative Arts Toi Rauwhārangi, Massey University. Her work involves the creation of clothes that have the ears, tails and fur of other-ly creatures, which she then wears on hiking trips into the forest. These performances are archived, and a source for the narratives realised in her watercolours.

JANE SAYLE grew up on the south coast of Wellington. She has been a dealer in curios and ephemera, an art writer and reviewer, and a lecturer in art and design history. After living in California, France and Germany for ten years she returned to New Zealand in 2019. This is her first book of poems.

MASSEY
UNIVERSITY
PRESS

First published in 2021 by
Massey University Press
Private Bag 102904
North Shore Mail Centre
Auckland 0745, New Zealand
www.masseypress.ac.nz

Photographs of
Catherine Bagnall's paintings
by Richard Reddaway

Design:
Anna Brown & Jo Bailey
Cover artwork:
Catherine Bagnall,
Lightness, 2013

A catalogue record for this book is available from the National Library of New Zealand

Printed and bound in China by Everbest Printing Investment Limited

ISBN: 978-0-9951378-2-0